ROCKFORD PUBLIC LIBRARY

3 1112 01477974 4

J 736.982 BOO
Boonyadhistarn, Thiranut
Origami : the fun and
funky art of paper folding

081406

ROCKFORD PUBLIC LIBRARY

Rockford, Illinois

www.rockfordpubliclibrary.org

815-965-9511

WITHDRAWN

WITHDRAWN

Origami

The Fun and Funky Art of Paper Folding

by Thiranut Boonyadhistarn

Capstone press

Mankato, Minnesota

ROCKFORD PUBLIC LIBRARY

Snap Books are published by Capstone Press,
151 Good Counsel Drive, P.O. Box 669, Mankato, Minnesota 56002.
www.capstonepress.com

Copyright © 2007 by Capstone Press. All rights reserved.
No part of this publication may be reproduced in whole or in part, or stored
in a retrieval system, or transmitted in any form or by any means,
electronic, mechanical, photocopying, recording, or otherwise, without
written permission of the publisher.
For information regarding permission, write to Capstone Press,
151 Good Counsel Drive, P.O. Box 669, Dept. R, Mankato, Minnesota 56002.
Printed in the United States of America

Library of Congress Cataloging-in-Publication Data

Boonyadhistarn, Thiranut.

    Origami: the fun and funky art of paper folding / by Thiranut Boonyadhistarn.

    p. cm. — (Snap books. Crafts)

    Summary: "A do-it-yourself crafts book for children and pre-teens on origami"—Provided by publisher.

    Includes bibliographical references and index.

    ISBN-13: 978-0-7368-6476-3 (hardcover)

    ISBN-10: 0-7368-6476-8 (hardcover)

    1. Origami—Juvenile literature. I. Title. II. Series.

TT870.B59 2007

736'.982—dc22

2006004099

Editor: Megan Schoeneberger
Designer: Bobbi J. Wyss
Production Artist: Renée T. Doyle
Illustrator: Thiranut Boonyadhistarn
Photo Researcher: Kelly Garvin

Photo Credits:
Aubrey Whitten, 32; Capstone Press/Karon Dubke, cover (objects), 4–5, 5 (right), 6, 7, 9, 10 (all), 11, 13 (all), 14, 15, 17, 18–19, 19 (right), 21, 22, 24–25, 27 (all); Getty Images/Hulton Archive/Stringer, 28 (left); Photodisc/Barbara Penoyar, cover (girl)

1 2 3 4 5 6 11 10 09 08 07 06

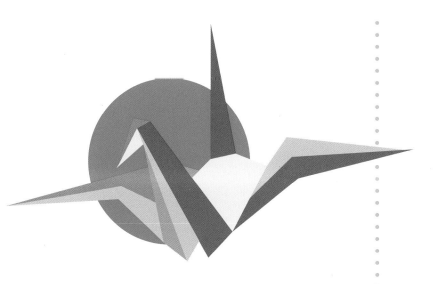

Table of Contents

Go Metric!

It's easy to change measurements
to metric! Just use this chart.

To change	into	multiply by
inches	centimeters	2.54
inches	millimeters	25.4
feet	meters	.305
yards	meters	.914
ounces (liquid)	milliliters	29.57
ounces (liquid)	liters	.029
cups (liquid)	liters	.237
pints	liters	.473
quarts	liters	.946
gallons	liters	3.78
ounces (dry)	grams	28.35
pounds	grams	453.59

CHAPTER 1

Pass the Paper

Origami is the Japanese word for paper folding.

We use paper at school and at home for all sorts of things. We use it to wrap presents, do homework assignments, and write notes to friends. Now you can learn to make fun folded models from it. Origami will put a whole new spin on paper for you.

That's it! For starters, stick with medium-sized paper, about 6 inches by 6 inches. With practice, you might try smaller or larger sheets. The only other materials you will need include glue for the two-part models in Chapter 4 and Chapter 5, and some craft items to decorate your models.

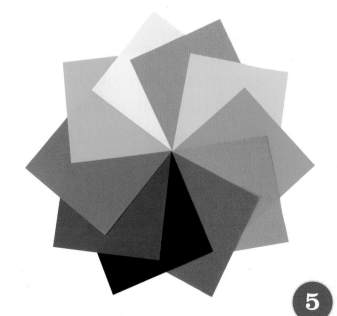

CHAPTER 2

Pick a Pack of Paper

So much paper, so little time.

When you hit the stores, you'll find a bunch of different kinds of paper. **Irogami** is the most common type of origami paper. This paper is colored or patterned on one side and white on the other. You can buy irogami and other origami papers at art supply stores, stationery stores, and some Internet stores.

Protect Your Paper

Always store origami paper flat and in dry conditions. Keep your favorite papers safe by storing them in an acid-free **archival box.** This type of box will prevent the colors from bleeding or fading. You can buy archival boxes at stores that carry scrapbooking or photo supplies.

But you don't have to buy specialty paper to do origami. Make your own square sheets from ordinary 8½-inch by 11-inch paper. Just fold one side of the paper diagonally to meet the other side. Cut off the extra strip at the bottom, and you will have a square sheet. Now start folding!

Go Paper Crazy!

You can find origami papers in more colors and styles than you can imagine.

- animal prints
- double-sided
- dyed
- flower prints
- **hologram paper**
- nature prints
- optical illusion
- polka dots
- solid colors
- stripes
- transparent
- **washi**

CHAPTER 3

Follow That Sign

What do all those symbols mean?

Do all the lines, dots, and dashes on origami diagrams make you dizzy? Don't worry. It's easy to learn origami symbols. This book also has written instructions and lettered diagrams to keep you folding in the right direction.

A dashed line means to **valley-fold** the paper. The fold goes forward and ends up in front of or on top of the paper. Most folds in this book are valley folds.

- -

A line with dashes and dots means to **mountain-fold** the paper. This fold is toward the back of the paper and ends up behind or under the paper.

•—•—•—•—•—•—•—•—•—

A thin, solid line shows you where a **crease** is.

———————————————

A dotted line shows you *edges* on the other side of the paper that you can't see from the top view. Think of these lines as x-ray vision.

• •

A solid arrow shows you which direction to fold. You'll see these arrows for valley folds.

A half-arrow shows you which way to fold if you are folding the paper behind or under, as in a mountain fold.

A hollow arrow means to unfold an existing fold.

A line with a solid arrow on one end and a hollow arrow on the other means fold and then unfold the paper. You do this to form a crease.

A looped arrow means to turn the paper over.

Line 'Em Up!

When folding, always make sure sides and edges line up exactly. If you don't, your creation might not come out right.

Creasing also makes a huge difference. Make your creases very hard. Use your fingernail or a coin to make harder creases. Your models will hold their shape much better.

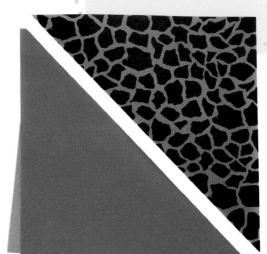

Great job!

Try better next time!

CHAPTER 4

Flower Power

These fabulous flowers can stay in bloom all year long.

You don't have a green thumb? Don't worry about it. You don't need dirt, water, or even sunshine for these lovely tulips to bloom. Fold these beautiful blossoms to give to friends and family members. Their faces will light up with joy. And unlike real flowers, these flowers last forever.

Getting on Base!

A **base** is a series of simple folds to start off a bunch of different origami models. From the same base, you can make birds or flowers just by changing how you fold the rest of your model. Some of the bases you'll learn in this book are the Kite Base, the Preliminary Base, and the Pinwheel Base.

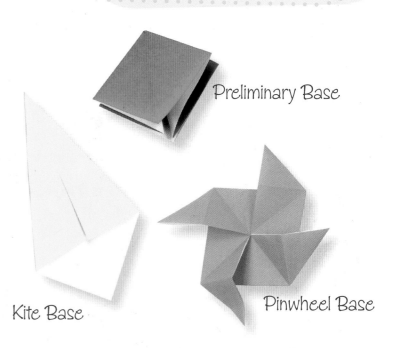

Preliminary Base

Kite Base

Pinwheel Base

Here's what you do

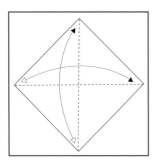

1 With white side up, fold in half, corner to corner, both ways. Unfold.

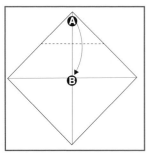

2 Valley-fold point A to point B.

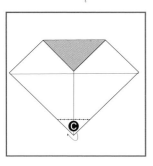

3 Mountain-fold point C behind paper.

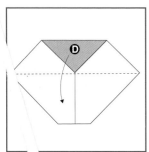

4 Valley-fold flap D on existing crease as shown.

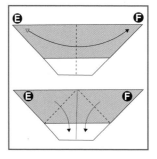

5 Valley-fold corner E to corner F to form crease, then unfold. Valley-fold corners E and F along the center crease.

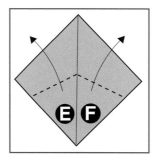

6 Valley-fold corners E and F as shown to form ears.

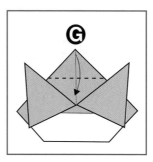

7 Valley-fold flap G down.

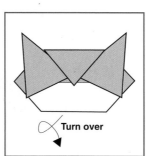

8 Turn the model over.

Turn over

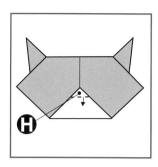

9 Valley-fold flap H to form the nose.

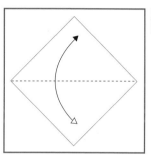

10 For the body, start with a new sheet of paper. With white side up, fold in half corner to corner to form center crease. Unfold.

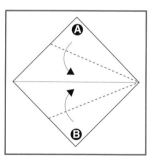

11 Valley-fold flaps A and B to center crease. You have now folded a Kite Base.

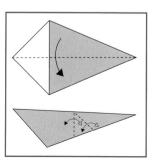

12 Valley-fold at center line. Then fold to form hard creases at lines shown. Hard creases will make the next step easier. Unfold.

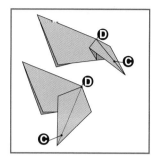

13 Lift flap C up and to the left. Squash down at point D and along the creases from step 12. This should form a little kite-shaped flap.

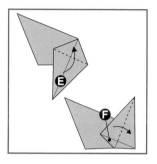

14 Valley-fold point E up. Valley-fold flap F to the right to form the tail. Glue the cat's head onto the body. Add some google eyes, rhinestones, or other decorations to your cat.

17

CHAPTER 6

Boxful of Goodies

These little paper boxes are perfect for storing your favorite candy, jewelry, or other small trinkets.

Now you've learned how to fold flowers and kittens. Let's move on to something you can really use. Keep your dresser, bedside table, or even your locker neat and organized with these pretty boxes. Or use them to hold little gifts for your friends and family throughout the year.

You Can Fold Anything

Folding fanatics will fold almost anything they can get their hands on. Business cards, sticky notes, gum wrappers, and even dollar bills—all of these can be made into fun origami models.

Here's what you do

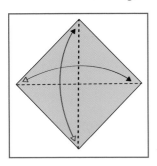

1 With color side facing up, valley-fold corner to corner both ways. Unfold.

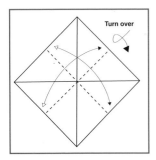

2 Turn over. Valley-fold side to side in each direction. Unfold.

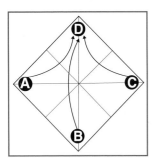

3 Pull points A, B, and C inward up to meet point D and flatten. This series of folds forms the Preliminary Base.

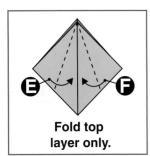

Fold top layer only.

4 Valley-fold flaps E and F (top layer only) to meet at center as shown.

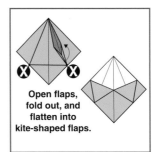

Open flaps, fold out, and flatten into kite-shaped flaps.

5 Open flaps slightly and squash at points X to flatten flaps. This fold will form kite-shaped flaps.

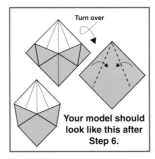

Turn over

Your model should look like this after Step 6.

6 Turn over. Repeat steps 4 and 5 on the other side.

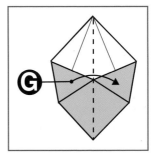

7 Valley-fold flap G (top layer only) to the right.

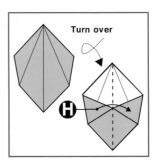

Turn over

8 Turn over. Valley-fold flap H (top layer only) to the right.

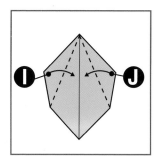

9 Valley-fold flaps I and J to center as shown.

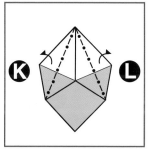

10 Mountain-fold flaps K and L to center as shown.

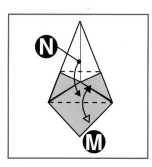

11 Fold and unfold flap M to make a crease. Valley-fold flap N down.

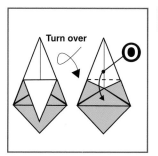

12 Turn over. Valley-fold flap O down.

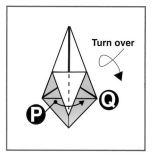

13 Valley-fold flap P (top layer only) to flap Q. Turn over and repeat.

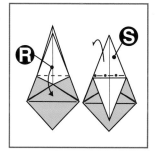

14 Valley-fold flap R down, and mountain-fold flap S behind model.

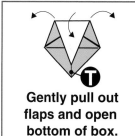

Gently pull out flaps and open bottom of box.

15 Gently push up point T while carefully pulling out the four points.

21

CHAPTER 7

Beyond the Sea

Something's fishy here!

These fish don't need any water. Just fold them and put them in a fishbowl with some glass marbles. You'll never have to remember to feed them or change their icky water.

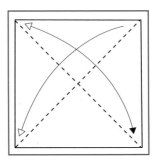

1 With white side facing up, valley-fold corner to corner both ways. Unfold.

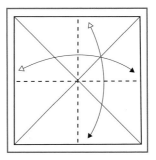

2 Valley-fold side to side both ways. Unfold.

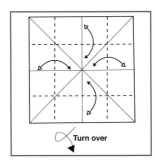

3 Valley-fold to form creases where shown. Unfold. Turn paper over.

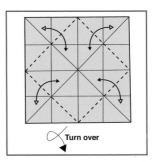

4 With color side facing up, fold in corners to center point. Unfold. Turn paper over again.

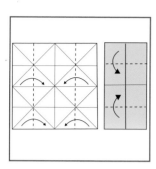

5 Valley-fold side flaps in to the center line. Valley-fold top and bottom flaps in to the center line.

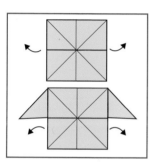

6 Pull out the corners of the top flaps and flatten. Pull out the corners of the bottom flaps and flatten.

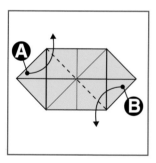

7 Valley-fold flap A up and flap B down. You have now folded the Pinwheel Base.

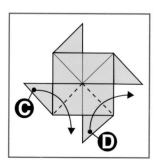

8 Valley-fold flap C down and flap D out to the side.

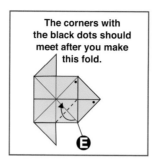

The corners with the black dots should meet after you make this fold.

9 Valley-fold flap E up so that the two black dots meet.

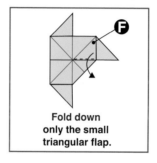

Fold down only the small triangular flap.

10 Valley-fold the small triangular flap F down.

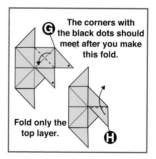

The corners with the black dots should meet after you make this fold.

Fold only the top layer.

11 Valley-fold flap G down. Valley-fold flap H up.

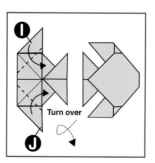

Turn over

12 Valley-fold flaps I and J where shown. Turn model over, and your fish is ready to swim.

23

CHAPTER 8

Still Soaring

The paper crane is the most beloved of all origami models.

The paper crane is a symbol of peace, hope, and love. It is one of the first models children in Japan learn to fold. It might seem a little tricky at first, so use throwaway paper to start. With practice, you'll find it's one of the easier projects to fold.

Crane Earrings

You'll need 3-inch by 3-inch paper for these dangling beauties. You can use smaller paper if you think you can fold it. You'll also need:

- $\frac{1}{16}$-inch hole punch
- needlenose pliers
- 2 jump rings, 6-millimeter size
- 2 ear hooks

Fold two cranes. Punch a hole near the top of the body on each crane. Use the pliers to open a gap in each jump ring. Loop each jump ring through a crane and an ear hook. Use the pliers to close up each ring. Now put the earrings on and let them fly.

Fast Facts

The Magic of Paper

American magician and escape artist Harry Houdini was a big fan of origami. In 1922, he wrote a book called *Paper Magic*. The book included instructions for folding several origami models including the Flapping Bird.

That's One Big Bird

The *Guinness Book of World Records* has recognized only one origami feat. The largest crane ever folded had a wingspan that stretched more than 256 feet. It took 1,000 people in Odate City, Japan, to fold it in January 2001.

The Godfather of Origami

Akira Yoshizawa was the modern master of origami. By the time he died at age 94, he had created more than 50,000 origami models. He also wrote 18 origami books and came up with the origami symbols we still use today.

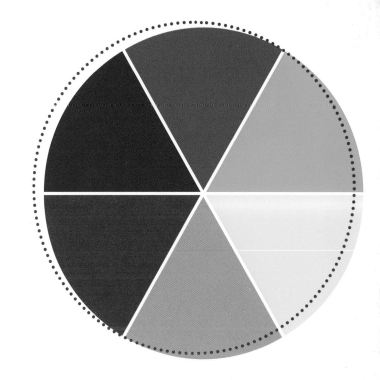

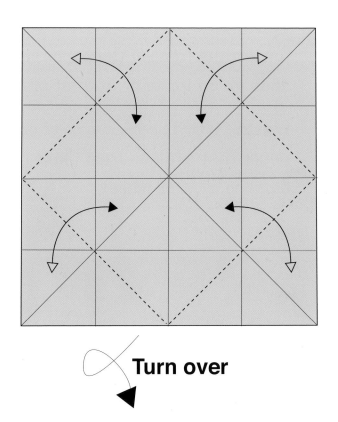

Turn over

Color Wheel

Is color important for origami? If you're folding something to be part of a set or to decorate your room, then yes. Understanding the color wheel may help you decide which papers to use together. On the wheel, the colors next to each other work together in harmony. Colors opposite each other have a stronger effect when used together because they have more contrast.

Glossary

archival box (ar-KIVE-uhl BOKS)— a box for storing photographs and papers so that they don't fade or get damaged

base (BAYSS)—a simple series of folds that can lead to more than one model

crease (KREESS)—a line or ridge made by folding a material such as paper

hologram paper (HOL-uh-gram PAY-pur)—a type of origami paper that has a shiny pattern with a three-dimensional effect

irogami (ihr-uh-GAH-mee)—a type of origami paper that is colored on one side and white on the other; irogami is the most common type of origami paper.

mountain-fold (MOUN-tuhn-FOHLD)— to fold toward the back of the paper so that it ends up underneath or behind itself

valley-fold (VAL-ee-FOHLD)—to fold toward the front of the paper so that it ends up on top of or in front of itself

washi (WOSH-ee)—a type of origami paper that is made from plant fibers, bamboo, rice, or wheat

Read More

Berry, Thiranut Deborah. *Origami for Fun!* For Fun! Minneapolis: Compass Point Books, 2005.

Gleason, Katherine A. *Friendship Origami.* Lake Mary, Fla.: Tangerine Press/Scholastic, 2004.

Johnson, Anne Akers. *Origami.* Palo Alto, Calif.: Klutz, 2004.

Montroll, John. *Dollar Bill Origami.* Mineola, New York: Dover, 2003.

Smith, Soonboke. *Origami for the First Time.* New York: Sterling, 2003.

Internet Sites

FactHound offers a safe, fun way to find Internet sites related to this book. All of the sites on FactHound have been researched by our staff.

Here's how:

1. Visit *www.facthound.com*
2. Choose your grade level.
3. Type in this book ID **0736864768** for age-appropriate sites. You may also browse subjects by clicking on letters, or by clicking on pictures and words.
4. Click on the **Fetch It** button.

FactHound will fetch the best sites for you!

About the Author

Thiranut Boonyadhistarn grew up in Tokyo, Bangkok, and Chicago. She learned various crafts in each country: origami in Japan, beading in Thailand, and paper crafts in America. The crafts she learned as a child have led to a lifelong love of the arts.

Boonyadhistarn has worked in film and TV production, graphic design, and book production. She also has written several kids' books on crafts. She lives in a tiny apartment in New York City, surrounded by boxes of glitter, rhinestones, and craft glue.

Index